Your Career Resilience Blueprint

A Tactical Guide to Navigate Change, Overcome Obstacles, and Design Your Future

CINDY GOODWIN-SAK AND MELISSA COHEN

Copyright © 2024 by Cindy Goodwin-Sak and Melissa Cohen

All rights reserved. No part of this publication may be reproduced, stored, or transmitted in any form or by any means, electronic, mechanical, photocopying, recording, scanning, or otherwise, without written permission from the publisher. It is illegal to copy this book, post it to a website, or distribute it by any other means without permission.

Cindy Goodwin-Sak and Melissa Cohen are not responsible for the persistence or accuracy of URLs for external or third-party Internet websites referred to in this publication and do not guarantee that any content on such websites is, or will remain, accurate or appropriate.

First Edition

Contents

I. WHO ARE YOU AND WHERE ARE YOU GOING?...................1
- You Deserve the Career You Desire 3
- Be Unique 9
- Identify Your Values 15
- Career Vision - Beyond Titles................................... 23
- Beyond the Corporate Ladder.................................... 31

II. WHAT SKILLS AND NETWORK DO YOU NEED? 43
- Skill Gaps... 45
- Network Gaps.. 51
- Stand-Out Personal Brand 57
- Feedback 69

III. GOAL... PLAN... EXECUTE! 75
- Goals 77
- Build Your Plan 87
- Expanding Your Skillset 93
- Power Skills 105
- Mentors & Sponsors 113

IV. TROUBLESHOOTING 131
- Organizational Politics...................................... 133
- Navigating Challenges & Setbacks 141
- Next Steps 147
- References 149

Acknowledgments

A huge thank you and a special call-out to some incredible supporters: Ari Weinstein, Michelle Ferguson, Eugina Jordan, Ricki Pasinelli, Lyndsay Dowd, Mahdi Hassan, Julie Morris, Eden Ezell, Charity Hughes, Leslie Nydick, Deborah Brown-Volkman, Alissa Randall, Leigh Burgess, Erin O'Mara, Kimberly Arnold, Michelle Bufano, Shelly Blackburn, Pamela Ottaway, Cathy Kearns, Diane Cooley, and Krista Seeman.

From Melissa: Special thanks to Mom and Dad, and to Doug and Chloe. Thank you for all your love and support. I love you very much!

From Cindy: Brian, you're my rock and the love of my life. Thank you. Caden and Maya, I'm so excited to watch you transform into the humans you want to be. I'm cheering for you!

Preface

If you're a first or second-line manager, this book is for you. For a couple of generations, companies created long-term incentives such as pensions to encourage employees to stay. These employees valued this investment, so they stuck with their jobs even if they weren't promoted. Corporate environments are entirely different today than they were even 50 years ago. In the face of massive technology advancements, they must continuously reinvent themselves to remain competitive. There are also entirely different expectations from shareholders today than we've seen before. This has dramatically shifted corporate incentives as well as corporate "loyalty" to their employees.

Employees are rarely seen as strategic assets in corporations today. Instead, they are resources: a means to an end. Layoffs are frequent. In some corporations, we see rolling layoffs, or more than one per year. This is a normal part of operations. As this becomes the norm, we want to arm you with the strategies to build a resilient career. Not only resilient, but the one YOU want and desire.

Too many leaders will tell you, "I've never applied for a job. I've always been tapped on the shoulder." This is generally a lie. They've followed a strategy similar to the one in this book, but either don't recognize it, or aren't sharing their strategy. We're here to share the secret of having the career you desire. While this book was written for first and second-line managers, it's actually a tool for anyone and everyone who is interested in building a resilient career.

How to Use This Book

This book is your interactive companion on your career resilience journey. We've packed it with practical exercises, insightful prompts, and valuable resources to help you navigate the complexities of the professional world.

Here's how to make the most of this book:
1. **Engage with the Exercises** - Throughout the chapters, you'll find thought-provoking exercises designed to help you uncover your strengths, clarify your goals, and develop your skills. Take the time to complete these exercises thoughtfully and honestly. They are your key to unlocking the full potential of this book.
2. **Scan the QR Codes** - We've included QR codes throughout the book to give you instant access to additional resources, including printable worksheets, fillable PDFs, and online tools. Simply use your smartphone or tablet to scan the codes and unlock a treasure trove of supplementary materials.
3. **Explore the Links** - We've also embedded links to articles, videos, and other online resources that can further enrich your learning experience. These links offer additional perspectives, practical tips, and inspiring stories to support your career journey.
4. **Make it Your Own** - This book is meant to be personalized. Feel free to highlight key passages, jot down notes in the margins, and make it your own. The more you interact with the material, the more valuable it will become.
5. **Take Action** - The ultimate goal of this book is to empower you to take action and create the career you desire. Don't just read the words; apply the principles, implement the strategies, and watch your career flourish.

Your efforts here will pay huge dividends in no time.

I. Who are you and where are you going?

If you're reading this book, you likely feel
a little stuck or lost in navigating your career.
Not to worry.
So many before you have felt the same.

The difference?
You're taking action!

This book is full of tested ways to get you unstuck
and pointed in the right direction for
a meaningful and fulfilling leadership career.

Let's get started!

"You do not find the happy life.
You make it."
- Camilla Eyring Kimball

1

You Deserve the Career You Desire

You've always been someone who goes after what you want, a real visionary. You climb the ranks, set ambitious goals, and crush them. But lately, there's this feeling - a knot in your stomach, a nagging doubt. You look around at the familiar walls of your office, the faces of your team, and it all feels static. You're stuck.

Maybe the projects have lost their shine. The meetings, once exciting, now feel like endless cycles of the same conversations. Your inbox is a black hole of tasks that don't inspire. The thrill of the chase, the joy of innovation – it's all dulled.

You're questioning your choices and your values. Are you on the right track? Is this what you truly want? You look at your peers, those who seem to glide up the ladder effortlessly, and wonder if you've missed a step. You question your abilities and your worth.

People around you are getting promoted. You've gone for a new job, but not received it. Instead, you get feedback that "you were in the top two, and the other candidate simply had more experience." Your boss is in the same position they took three to five years ago and is showing no signs of moving up, so that path is blocked.

The frustration simmers beneath the surface. It seeps into your conversations, your decisions, your relationships. You snap at your team, withdraw from social gatherings, and find solace in late-night work sessions that yield diminishing returns.

But amid the frustration and doubt, there's a flicker of hope. A quiet voice that whispers of possibility, of change. It reminds you of your resilience, your creativity, your unwavering spirit. It urges you to explore the unknown, to step outside your comfort zone, to embrace the uncertainty that lies ahead.

The path may not be clear, but it's there. It's waiting for you to take the first step. To break free from the chains of stagnation, to rediscover your passion, to rewrite your story. It's time to rise above the limitations, to unleash your true potential, to create a future that fills you with purpose and joy.

This book is designed to be your catalyst – the spark that ignites your transformation. With practical strategies, insightful exercises, and proven techniques, it will empower you to:

Uncover your hidden strengths - Discover the skills, passions, and experiences that make you unique and valuable.

Define your ideal career path - Gain clarity on the type of work that will bring you fulfillment and align with your long-term goals.

Break through limiting beliefs - Challenge the doubts and fears that have been keeping you stuck.

Create a powerful action plan - Develop a roadmap of tangible steps that will propel you toward the career you desire.

This isn't just about navigating your career – it's about stepping into your full potential and achieving the level of success you know you're capable of.

> **Pro Tip: This book is designed for you to work through your strategy. Take your time and do the exercises. We promise it will pay significant dividends.*

Books come in all shapes and sizes. This one comes with a companion PDF for documenting your thoughts electronically or a journal you can print. Everywhere you see this symbol…

…you'll find a corresponding exercise in the PDF or journal. While you may like the convenience of digital, research shows that handwriting activates more areas of the brain for learning and memory than typing.[i] No excuses! Grab your favorite medium, or just write here in the book. It's okay. We'll wait for you.

https://is.gd/printpdf	*https://is.gd/fillable*
Printable PDF	**Fillable PDF**

One more bit of advice from two of us who have been in your shoes. The path to a fulfilling career isn't always a smooth one. It's paved with doubts, fears, and the nagging feeling that you might not be enough. Perhaps you've hesitated to pursue a promotion, convinced that you're not truly qualified, or the thought of stepping outside your comfort zone sends shivers down your spine. Maybe you've even asked yourself, "Am I an imposter?"

If you can relate to these thoughts, know that you are not alone. Imposter syndrome, risk aversion, and the fear of failure often accompany the journey to success. But here's the secret: you don't have to overcome these feelings to move forward. You can bring them along on the journey.

This book is your invitation to acknowledge your fears, embrace your vulnerabilities, and step boldly into the unknown. It's a recognition that your doubts don't disqualify you; they simply highlight the areas where you can grow. It's a call to action to use your fear as fuel, to let it drive you toward the challenges that will ultimately shape you into the leader you're meant to be.

Remember, every successful leader (at least the ones others want to work for) has faced moments of uncertainty and self-doubt. The difference lies in their willingness to push through those feelings, to take calculated risks, and to never stop learning. So, let this book be your guide, cheerleader, and toolkit as you embark on this exciting journey of career resilience. Embrace the discomfort, celebrate the victories, and never lose sight of the incredible potential that lies within you.

Let's do this!

"Be yourself; everyone else is already taken."
- Oscar Wilde

2

Be Unique

When you're looking for a leadership role, it's easy to fall into the trap of highlighting the same skills that everyone else does. But to stand out from the crowd, you need to focus on your unique strengths. What makes you different from everyone else? What special talents or abilities do you have that can help you succeed in this role?

Unique Experiences

There is no one else on the planet with experiences identical to you. You are truly one-of-a-kind. So, what can you bring from these experiences to a new leadership role that will make you uniquely qualified for the job?

Your individual blend of experiences, whether from diverse industries, unusual hobbies, or challenging life events, has equipped you with a perspective that others don't have. This allows you to approach problems creatively, anticipate unexpected challenges, and connect with a wider range of people. In a leadership role, this translates to innovative solutions, adaptable strategies, and the ability to build a truly inclusive team.

Every experience, from successes to setbacks, has contributed to your personal and professional growth. The skills you've honed, the lessons you've learned, and the resilience you've developed are invaluable assets in a leadership position. These experiences have likely made you a stronger communicator, a more empathetic listener, and a more decisive decision-maker – all essential qualities for a successful leader.

Even experiences that appear unrelated to your desired leadership role likely hold hidden value. The skills you've acquired, whether it's managing a household budget, organizing a community event, or navigating a complex software system, are transferable to a leadership context. Perhaps you've mastered the art of conflict resolution, honed your negotiation skills, or discovered a talent for motivating others. These transferable skills can make you a surprisingly effective leader in a new and unfamiliar environment.

When Cindy was applying for her first manager role, a mentor asked her a phenomenal question. "What are the three qualities you possess that make you uniquely qualified for the role." This question set the foundation for her to think differently about each position. Rather than trying to conform to everyone else's expectations, she realized that the secret was standing out from the crowd.

The key is to identify *your* hidden strengths – the experiences, skills, and perspectives that have uniquely shaped you. Roll up your sleeves - we're digging in!

Dig Deeper than Your Resume

Your resume is a snapshot of your titles and accomplishments, but it doesn't come close to telling the whole story. Think about the challenges you've overcome, both professionally and personally:

Have you successfully navigated a company merger, a difficult team dynamic, or a complex project with tight deadlines? Your resilience speaks to your leadership potential.

Were you an early advocate for a new technology, a process improvement, or a push for diversity and inclusion? Your ability to drive change is a leadership asset.

Don't underestimate the transferable skills gained outside of work. Parenting, volunteer experiences, or overcoming personal challenges all shape your ability to empathize, problem-solve, and inspire.

✏️ 2.1

Document your experiences here:

_____

_____

_____

_____

_____

Analyze Your "Wow" Moments

Think about times in your career when you exceeded a sales target, delivered a project ahead of schedule, or turned around a struggling team's performance. Analyze what you did differently that contributed to this success.

Think back to specific feedback you've received. Were you commended for your creativity, your ability to motivate others, or your strategic thinking?

When did you feel most energized and 'in the zone'? These are clues to activities you naturally excel in and bring out your best leadership qualities.

Write your "wow" moments below. If you're struggling, think of it just as documenting the facts.

_____

_____

_____

_____

_____

Get an Outsider's Perspective

Sometimes, we're blind to our own strengths. Ask a trusted mentor, colleague, or friend:

- "What are my biggest strengths that I might overlook?"
- "Can you give an example of a time when you saw me demonstrate leadership potential?"
- "What do you see as my unique experiences that (could) contribute to my perspective as a leader?"

Write the feedback you've received below so that you have a place to compare it with your reflections.

_____

_____

_____

_____

_____

Incorporating your unique experiences and strengths into your career vision can help you stand out as a candidate for a leadership role. You can position yourself as a valuable and distinctive leader in any new environment by highlighting what sets you apart from others and embracing your diverse skill set.

> **Pro Tip: Some people have trouble with this because they feel like they're proclaiming themselves to be better than others. We struggled with this ourselves. This exercise is all about the unique combination of skills that make you most capable of taking a team to the next level at any given time. If you have trouble with this, work with a friend to identify and practice sharing them.*

"It's not hard to make decisions when you know what your values are."
– Roy Disney

3

Identify Your Values

Before you decide what you want from your career, it's important to know your core values. These are things that are most important to you and influence how you make decisions, act, and interact with people. They shape your beliefs, what you care about, and how you live your life. Identifying your core values can help you be clearer about what you want and live a life that feels good to you. In this section, we'll help you uncover your values so you can set career goals that match who you are and who you want to be.

We've worked with so many leaders who don't understand this until they're well into their careers. Going through the motions without understanding your core values can create significant stress in your life. It did for us. Do yourself a favor and do the work in this section. Your future self will thank you.

Experiences and Influences

Think about the times when you felt like you were on top of the world. You know, those moments when everything just seemed to click, and you felt like you could do anything? Those are called "peak experiences." We want more of these experiences in our careers and in our lives.

On the flip side, there are also those times when life throws you a curve ball and you feel like you're at the bottom of the barrel. Those are the "painful experiences." We'll continue to experience them, but we want to minimize them and learn from all the previous ones.

But here's the thing: both experiences can teach you quite a bit about yourself. When you think about what made those moments so special or so difficult, you can understand what's truly important to you. What makes you feel alive? What kind of people do you want to surround yourself with? What kind of work do you want to do?

As Cindy and Melissa climbed the corporate ladder, they discovered that their negative experiences often fueled their strongest values. They also have found their values shifting throughout their careers. This is entirely normal.

So, take some time to reflect on your good and bad experiences and see if you can start to identify patterns. Those patterns might lead you to your core values.

✏️ 3.1

_____

_____

_____

_____

_____

> *Pro Tip: Pay attention to the areas where you are unwilling to compromise. Those are probably some of your most important values.*

Create a List of Potential Values

Let's start by drafting a comprehensive list of values that resonate with you. This list can include qualities like compassion, creativity, independence, loyalty, or ambition. Don't worry about narrowing it down just yet—this is about brainstorming and recognizing what speaks to you. You can find lists of values to start with, but feel free to add any that may not be included. On the next page, you'll find a list of values to get you started. Please don't limit yourself to this list. Highlight, circle, cross out, and do anything you need to identify those that resonate with you.

 3.2

Accountability	Generosity	Open-Mindedness
Achievement	Gratitude	Optimism
Ambition	Growth	Security
Balance	Happiness	Personal Development
Caring	Health/Well-Being	Professionalism
Collaboration	Honesty	Punctuality
Compassion	Humility	Recognition
Courage	Knowledge	Relationships
Creativity	Individuality	Reliability
Curiosity	Innovation	Resilience
Dependability	Integrity	Respect
Empathy	Joy	Responsibility
Enthusiasm	Justice	Risk-Taking
Excellence	Kindness	Security
Fairness	Knowledge	Self-control
Family	Learning	Service
Flexibility	Love	Spirituality
Freedom	Loyalty	Stability
Friendships	Making a Difference	Success
Fun	Motivation	Wealth

Other Values Not Listed Above

_____ _____

_____ _____

_____ _____

_____ _____

_____ _____

Narrow Down Your List

Once you have your list, start narrowing it down to your top five to ten values. This process requires thoughtful consideration; compare each value against the others and think about which ones are truly essential to your identity and happiness. Consider using a ranking system or asking yourself hypothetical scenarios to determine which values are non-negotiable.

Top Values (up to 10)

_____   _____

_____   _____

_____   _____

_____   _____

_____   _____

With your shortened list, take some time to reflect on each value. How do these values show up in your life currently? Are there values you wish to embody more fully? It's important to remember that your core values should represent who you are, not who you think you should be. Be honest with yourself, and don't be afraid to revise your list if something doesn't feel right.

> **Pro Tip: If you really want to get to know your values, limit yourself to five-to-seven and stack rank them. You can do this by comparing each value and choosing one over the other. It's like a college basketball tournament, but this is the Tournament of Values!*

Tournament of Values

Core Values

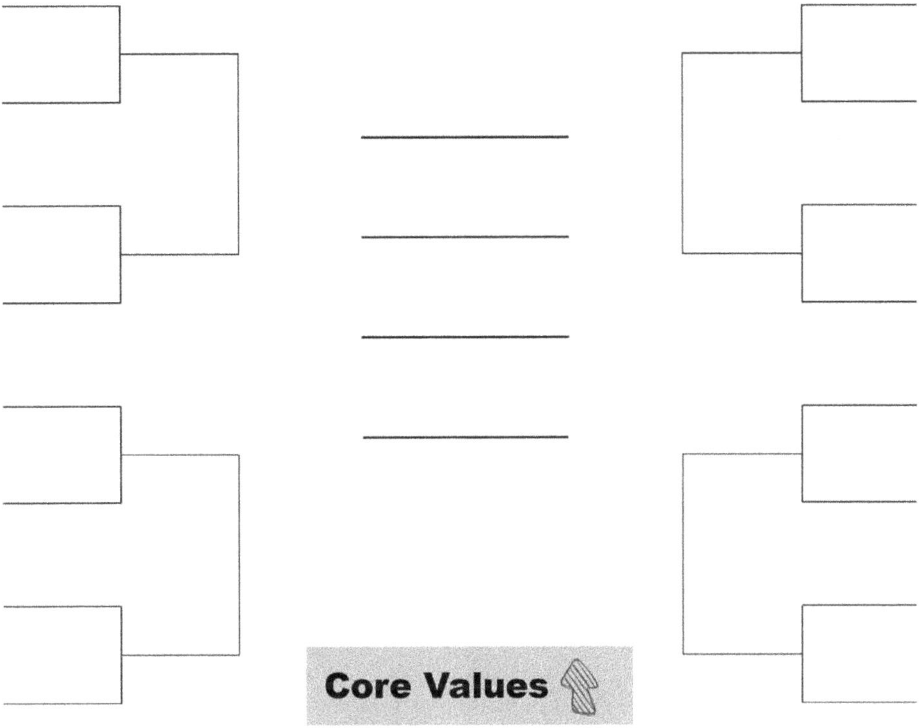

Now that you have your list of values, we will use this list frequently. We've provided a page for you to print with your values and goals in one location. That is in Chapter 10 or in the downloadable notebook. Use this to keep your values and goals handy in your planners, by your computer, or anywhere that you might be making decisions. These values and goals should drive most of your decisions.

"Vision without action is merely a dream. Action without vision just passes time. Vision with action can change the world."
- Joel A. Barker

4

Career Vision - Beyond Titles

Melissa's first corporate job made her feel extremely proud. She had landed a role with a well-known fashion brand; she felt on top of the world. However, she soon learned that her manger - just one level above her - had been with the organization for twenty-five years. This was a concern.

If her boss had been there for over two decades and was only one level above her, what did that mean for the opportunities to advance within the company? After two years and taking time to reflect on what she wanted, this was ultimately a driving factor for Melissa's decision to look outside the organization and take a role with another company.

Many people we've spoken with have been in the same industry for years and still haven't moved up from manager. Often, they stay in the same role, waiting for their boss to move. Other times, they're moving around to new opportunities without a plan. Don't be like them! Have a vision so you know each move is moving you toward your goals.

Now that you understand what makes you unique and what you truly value, it's time to create a vision for your career that's meaningful and unique to you. It's not about attaining a specific title. It's about the work you want to do, the people you want to do it with, and how it integrates into your life. We'll help you steer clear of the trap of focusing solely on traditional job titles and focus instead on what you really want out of your professional life.

Understanding the Scope of Your Work

Think about what really excites you about your career. What industry or field do you feel passionate about? Consider the problems you want to solve or the contributions you want to make. For Cindy, she wanted to travel the world, better understand other cultures and how they do business, to influence product direction and team strategies. Above all, she wanted to inspire and lead large teams of people with diverse skills and expertise.

Travel was important to Melissa as well. At a certain point in her career, she became frustrated that all of the travel was being done by her boss. When her boss went on maternity leave, Melissa was finally able to take a trip overseas, and that solidified how important this piece was for her own development. When she looked for her next opportunity, she asked about travel in interviews. Travel was a big deciding factor when ultimately accepting an offer. Visiting factories gave her a much better understanding of the manufacturing process and helped to solidify relationships with her overseas partners.

Now, imagine the companies, organizations, or communities you want to impact. Do you prefer working in a small or large team? Do you want to travel? Do you need to work in a specific city?

This step takes you beyond just job titles and helps you align your career vision with your values and interests.

> **Pro Tip: The rapid change of technology and policy means that new titles are emerging constantly.*
> *This is an excellent reason to keep your options open.*
> *You could be the pioneer of one of these roles.*
> *Do the work.*

4.1

_____
_____
_____
_____
_____

Visualize Your Day-to-Day

Picture your perfect workday from start to finish. What do you do during the day? Are you brainstorming new ideas, leading projects, mentoring others, or chatting with clients? By imagining your everyday activities, you can determine what you enjoy doing and which skills you want to use or develop. This exercise also shows you if you prefer collaborative or independent work, creative or analytical tasks, and routine or dynamic activities.

4.2

_____
_____
_____
_____
_____

Identify Your Collaborators

Consider the type of individuals you would like to collaborate with. Do you prefer working with creative minds or technically skilled individuals? Do you value working with people who are passionate about teaching or those who are community leaders? Additionally, think about whether you enjoy working in a team or if you prefer working independently. Understanding the type of people and relationships you want to cultivate can help you determine the ideal professional setting.

✎ 4.3

_____

_____

_____

_____

Defining Your Actions and Contributions

Think about what you want to do and achieve in your career. Are you working on projects that make a difference, creating new things to solve complicated problems, or telling stories that inspire people? This part of your vision connects what you do daily to the bigger impact you want to make, giving your work a sense of purpose and direction.

✏️ 4.4

___

Acknowledge What You're Not Doing

It's important to know what you don't want to do as much as what you want to do in your career. Take note of the things you want to avoid, such as boring office tasks, working in a super competitive environment, or a job that doesn't let you use your creative abilities. Being aware of these no-gos will help you figure out what you really want to do and keep you from crossing your limits.

✏️ 4.5

___

Non-Negotiables

One more thing to document before moving on to your career vision. What are your career and work non-negotiables? For Cindy, it was not moving after her kids were in grade school. She just couldn't handle the stress of the idea.

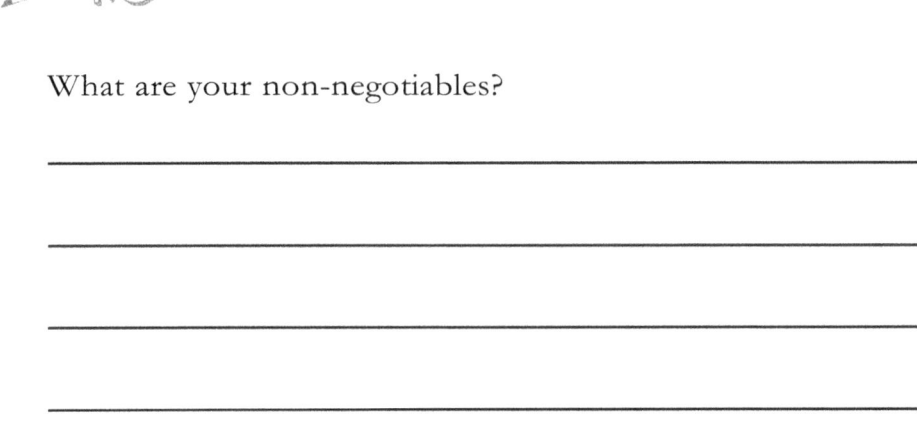

What are your non-negotiables?

_____

_____

_____

_____

_____

Bring Your Career Vision to Life

Using your thoughts above, start thinking about what you want to do in your career. Use descriptive words to create a picture of your ideal work life. Think about the type of work you'll do daily, the people you'll work with, and the impact you want to make. This vision should inspire you and guide your decisions when it comes to your career. It'll help you navigate challenges and find new opportunities. Remember to focus on the bigger picture and try to avoid specific job titles.

> *Pro Tip: This is one of the most critical exercises in this book. Truly understanding what work you want to do, the people you want to do it with, and how it works in your life is the most important thing you can do when setting a career vision. Use your core values to help you define the future YOU.*

Your Career Vision

What type of role might you have in 10-15 years? Avoid specific titles to the best of your ability. We know this is challenging, but it will greatly expand your options. This role may require two-to-four moves to achieve. By setting this career vision, you can ensure that the roles, skills, and experience you gain will move you ever closer to attaining your career vision.

✎ 4.7

_____

_____

_____

_____

"The only way to do great work is to love what you do. If you haven't found it yet, keep looking. Don't settle."
– Steve Jobs

5

Beyond the Corporate Ladder

The traditional way to advance a career and become a leader has been to climb the corporate ladder, which is generally straight and narrow. But things are changing, and many leaders these days are finding fulfillment and success in roles that are not part of the usual corporate structures. Whether they're looking for greater independence, aiming to make a difference in society, or simply looking for personal satisfaction, alternative career paths such as entrepreneurship, consulting, and non-profit leadership can provide outstanding opportunities for leaders to apply their skills and experiences in new and exciting ways.

We both knew long-term that we wanted a "second career" beyond corporate life. Corporate leadership can be phenomenal, but it can also be very taxing, both physically and emotionally. We wanted to make an impact in the corporate world and then use our expertise in a different way. That has led us both into a combination of entrepreneurship and consulting. We absolutely love our choices and have been intentional with those choices. *And* we went into our ventures, eyes wide open.

If you choose the same, we want you to know the benefits and challenges. So, let's dive in and take a closer look!

Entrepreneurship - Crafting Your Own Vision

Entrepreneurship is an enticing path for leaders looking to step out of traditional corporate roles and create something of their own. It offers the ultimate autonomy and the opportunity to directly reap the rewards of one's hard work and innovation.

Opportunities:

- **Autonomy and Freedom** - Entrepreneurs have the freedom to set their own schedules, choose their projects, and make strategic decisions about the direction of their business.
- **Creative Fulfillment** - Starting a business allows leaders to bring their ideas to life, from conceptualization to execution.
- **Financial Rewards** - Successful entrepreneurship can lead to significant financial gains, though it comes with risks.

Challenges:

- **Risk and Uncertainty** - Entrepreneurs face high levels of uncertainty and risk, particularly in the early stages of a business.
- **Resource Constraints** - Starting and growing a business requires significant resources, including time, money, and human capital.
- **Isolation** - Entrepreneurs often work alone or with a small team, which can be isolating compared to the collaborative environments of larger corporations.

If you think entrepreneurship might be for you, take a few moments to consider your idea and vet it below.

Self-Reflection

List your hobbies, interests, and activities you enjoy outside of work. What are you naturally drawn to? What topics could you talk about for hours?

✏️ 5.1

_____

_____

_____

_____

_____

✏️ 5.2

Identify your strengths and skills. What are you good at? What do people compliment you on? What unique abilities or knowledge do you possess?

_____

_____

_____

_____

_____

5.3

Think about problems you've encountered or observed in your experience. Are there any issues you'd like to solve or needs you'd like to meet?

_____

_____

_____

_____

Idea Generation

5.4

Look at your lists from Part 1 and identify areas where your passions and skills intersect. Are there any hobbies or interests that could be turned into a business? Could your skills be used to solve a problem or fulfill a need?

_____

_____

_____

_____

5.5

Spend some time brainstorming potential business ideas based on your passions, skills, experiences, and the problems you've identified. Don't hold back – write down every idea that comes to mind, no matter how wild or impractical it seems.

_____

_____

_____

_____

_____

5.6

Research your top ideas to see if there's a market for them. Are there similar businesses already operating? How would you differentiate yourself? What are the potential challenges and opportunities?

_____

_____

_____

_____

_____

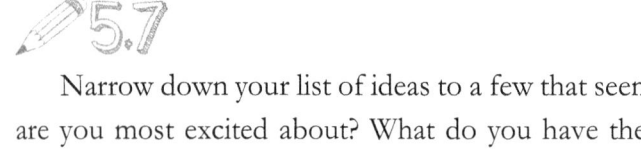

Narrow down your list of ideas to a few that seem most promising. What are you most excited about? What do you have the skills and resources to pursue?

_____

_____

_____

_____

_____

Additional Tips:
- Don't be afraid to think outside the box. Some of the most successful businesses started with unique or unconventional ideas.
- Talk to other entrepreneurs and get their feedback on your ideas.
- Be open to pivoting or changing your business idea as you learn more.

Consulting - Leveraging Your Expertise

Consulting offers another alternative for leaders seeking to escape the confines of traditional corporate roles. It allows you to leverage your expertise and provide advice and solutions to various organizations.

Opportunities:
- **Variety of Work** - Consultants have the opportunity to work with multiple clients across different industries, keeping their work dynamic and engaging.
- **Flexibility** - Consulting can offer more flexible working conditions than traditional corporate jobs, including the ability to set one's own hours and work from anywhere.
- **Professional Growth** - Working with diverse clients and on various projects can accelerate professional growth and learning.

Challenges:
- **Inconsistent Workload** - The demand for consulting services can be unpredictable, potentially leading to periods of high intensity followed by lulls.
- **Pressure to Deliver** - Consultants are expected to provide high-value advice and solutions, often under tight deadlines.
- **Building a Client Base** - Successful consulting requires a robust network and the ability to market oneself effectively to attract and retain clients.

Exploring Consulting

✏️ **5.8**

Identify Your Expertise. What are you exceptionally knowledgeable or skilled at? What topics do people often come to you for advice on? List three to five areas where you feel you have a strong base or knowledge and skill set.

_____

_____

_____

_____

_____

✏️ **5.9**

Passions. What aspects of your work do you find most engaging and fulfilling? What problems do you enjoy solving? Which industries or sectors excite you? List three to five areas that spark your interest and enthusiasm.

_____

_____

_____

_____

_____

5.10

Research the consulting landscape. Are there specific industries or areas where your expertise is in high demand? Identify two to three potential consulting niches where you could leverage your skills and knowledge.

_____

_____

_____

_____

_____

5.11

Consider your professional network. Do you have connections in industries or organizations where you could offer consulting services? Who could potentially be your first clients or refer you to others?

_____

_____

_____

_____

_____

Questions to Consider:

Are you comfortable with uncertainty and working on a project-by-project basis?

Are you willing to invest time and resources in marketing your services and building a client base?

Can you manage your time effectively and balance multiple projects simultaneously?

Are you comfortable with the idea of being your own boss and managing all aspects of your business?

_____

_____

_____

_____

Non-Profit Leadership - Making an Impact

Non-profit leadership can be a fulfilling alternative for leaders driven by a desire to make a social impact. This path allows individuals to apply their skills toward causes and missions they are passionate about.

Opportunities:

- **Social Impact** - Non-profit leaders can make a tangible

difference in their communities or in specific areas of interest, such as education, healthcare, or social justice.
- **Mission-Driven Work** - Working for a non-profit can provide a strong sense of purpose and fulfillment, as every aspect of the work is tied to the organization's mission.
- **Community and Relationships** - Non-profit leadership often involves building and nurturing relationships with volunteers, donors, and other stakeholders, creating a strong sense of community.

Challenges:

Resource Limitations - Non-profits often operate with limited resources, which can be a significant challenge for leaders used to corporate budgets.

Fundraising - A large part of non-profit leadership involves fundraising, which can be challenging and time-consuming.

Balancing Mission and Management - Non-profit leaders must balance the organization's mission with the realities of managing an organization, including budgeting, staffing, and strategic planning.

Questions to Consider

Would you be comfortable working in a resource-constrained environment?

Are you willing to prioritize mission impact over financial gain?

Can you envision yourself leading and inspiring a diverse team of staff and volunteers?

Are you prepared to navigate the complexities of fundraising and stakeholder management?

_____

_____

_____

_____

_____

> **Pro Tip: Nearly 60% of people consider changing careers in their life. The average age for people to change careers is 39. Remember this when you're thinking about the career you're building and climbing the corporate ladder vs other career options.[ii]*

You can succeed in your career in many ways without climbing the traditional corporate ladder. You can start your own business, work as a consultant, or lead a non-profit organization. Each of these options has its own unique challenges and rewards, so you need to think carefully before making a decision. But if you're willing to take a risk and try something new, you could find a fulfilling career that makes a difference. The most important thing is to find something that matches your values, skills, and interests, whether it's working in a company or out on your own.

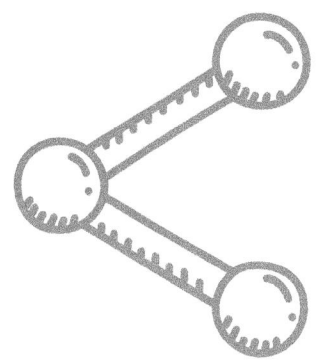

II. What skills and network do you need?

Now that you've explored the foundation, the skills you have, your unique value proposition, and where you're going, it's time to identify the skills and network you'll need to fulfill your vision.

Let's dive in!

"The illiterate of the 21st century will not be those who cannot read and write, but those who cannot learn, unlearn, and relearn."
– Alvin Toffler

6

Skill Gaps

Starting with your career vision, list the skills needed to get there. What are the differences between what you can do now and what you'll need to be able to do in the future? Do you need to be able to talk to people in a professional way? Do you need to be familiar with other cultures and the way business is done in other countries? Do you need to know how to lead a big team?

Cindy's skill gaps were mostly related to humans. As a "hard-core introvert with a little social anxiety" she struggled to make small-talk and understand how others operated. So, she focused on building her human skills. Melissa's biggest skill gap was understanding and experience working with other cultures. Many of her responsibilities involved working with people in other countries, countries she had never visited and whose cultures were very different from those in the United States. This was one of the reasons she prioritized the opportunity to travel when looking for the next role in her career. She wanted to immerse herself in these cultures to be more effective in her global roles.

Write your known skill gaps here:

_____

_____

_____

_____

_____

Conduct Informational Interviews

When you're trying to learn more about a particular career or industry, informational interviews can be a great way to connect with professionals who can give you an insider's view of the role and the skills, network, and brand needed.

Who to Interview?

Start by finding people who work in the jobs or fields you're interested in, and then send them a friendly message asking if they'd be willing to chat with you for a little bit. Make sure to emphasize that you're just looking for advice and not trying to land a job. Try to keep your meeting to 30 minutes or less and come up with a list of good questions beforehand, so you're ready to make the most of your time.

A great place to build your network is through LinkedIn, especially if you work remotely or are in a less-populated region. LinkedIn is a professional site available to everyone, so take advantage of the opportunity to meet people in the roles you desire and ask for introductions from shared connections. And remember, the lack of response from someone on LinkedIn is not a judgment of your character. Don't take it personally! People are busy, and not all people get notifications from LinkedIn. Patience and polite persistence are your friends. Most executive jobs aren't posted on public job boards. They are filled by executive searches, recruiters, or existing network connections. (See Network Gaps). With that information, reviewing job descriptions posted on public boards is still a good idea. However, we recommend that you consider only themes, not specifics.

We've found recruiters to be a great source of information. During other informational interviews, ask about which recruiters are focused in your area or the area where you wish to work. These interviews with recruiters are a great way to learn about future roles and build your network. Building relationships with professional recruiters is always a smart move.

> **Pro Tip: Don't forget to send a thank-you note after the interview to show your appreciation for their time.*

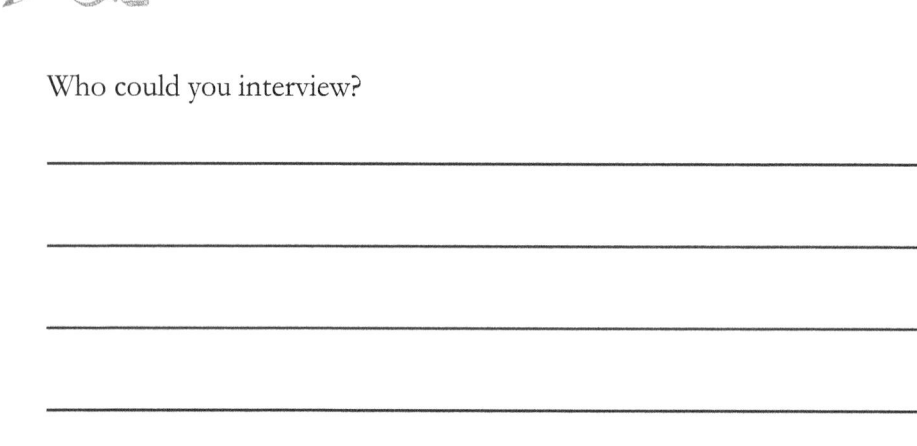

Who could you interview?

_____

_____

_____

_____

_____

How to do the Interview

When interviewing someone for information, actively listen to what they say and show a real interest in their opinions. Ask them what skills they think are important for the job and what additional things would make someone stand out. You could also ask about what's trending in the industry right now, and what type of jobs someone could get afterward. Thinking in terms of the steps, network, and opportunity a role can provide is critical to a strategic career. Finally, it may be worth asking if they are familiar with recruiters who could be helpful to you in your future job search.

6.3

Questions I'll ask:

_____

_____

_____

_____

_____

6.4

Consider what you learned and determine what skills and knowledge you need to improve. This will help you better understand what you need to succeed in your dream job, make new professional connections, and establish mentorship opportunities.

Document the skills and network learned from the interviews.

_____

_____

_____

_____

_____

"The richest people in the world look for and build networks, everyone else looks for work."
– Robert Kiyosaki

7

Network Gaps

"Your network is your net worth," is a famous quote by Tim Sanders, bestselling author and trainer. Even in a digital-first world, this statement holds true. The exact number of jobs that are obtained through networking is a hotly debated topic. If you go with the general rule that 70-85% of jobs are found through a network connection, it's probably not terribly far off.[iii]

Statistica reports that only 20% of jobs are filled from online applications, only one-fifth of total roles[iv]. It makes it a viable way to apply for jobs, but the statistics are against you.

Additionally, most corporations don't post vice president positions or above because of the overwhelming demand and number of unqualified candidates. But if the job isn't posted, how do you know about it? We'll give you one guess…

Given how important networking is for your career, you should have a structured plan and approach. Lucky for you, we've got tools to help you out!

Download our Stakeholder Tracking Sheet!

https://is.gd/stakeholdertracking

To build your own, create a spreadsheet that includes:
- Name, job title, company, and industry for each contact
- Note how you know each person (e.g., former colleague, alumni connection)
- Note on what interests they have

We like to use multiple tabs on our spreadsheet to help us organize our contacts. We recommend that you copy our spreadsheet and make it your own. We've created two tabs for you. You can duplicate our tabs, customize them, or create an entirely new sheet of your own. Some potential categories are:
- Job functions or roles
- Current or future contacts
- Geographical locations
- Inside my organization, outside my organization
- Professional Organizations

Now, document as many of the connections in your network as possible. These are peer-level or above. When was the last time you met with them? How important are they to your current and next roles? Who are you missing that might be important to know as you're progressing in your career? What value might you bring them?

Network Gaps

We're giving you space below to brainstorm on your connections. However, we strongly recommend using a spreadsheet for this. It gets complicated quickly, and you'll need a comprehensive reference point. You'll also need to update this sheet continuously with the last date of contact and notes about your connections. Be sure to check out our spreadsheet to get you up and running quickly!

7.1

_____

_____

_____

_____

_____

Now think far more broadly about your network. Studies show that it's your "weak links" that provide information about open positions. In 1973, researcher Mark Granovetter published "The Strength of Weak Ties." This was ground-breaking research into how people find jobs. It's not your close connections with whom you have frequent contact who help. It's your connections' connections. It's the people you don't know very well who help you find a role. We won't geek out over the reasons why. Just know that an article from 2023 shows that it hasn't changed a bit[v].

Who don't you know very well who might have insights into the types of roles that you're seeking?

_____

_____

_____

_____

_____

*Pro Tip: Just because you're an introvert doesn't mean that networking is impossible. Be thoughtful and intentional about the network you want to build. Invest your energy in the relationships that are most important to you. You can still be successful at networking AND be an introvert. Trust us. We know.

"Too many people overvalue what they are not and undervalue what they are."
– Malcolm S. Forbes

8

Stand-Out Personal Brand

Creating and boosting a personal brand is important for leaders who want to become more visible and appealing for higher-level roles. A strong personal brand not only distinguishes you in a crowded marketplace but also allows you to communicate your values, expertise, and unique qualities effectively.

What is a Personal Brand?

Most simply put, your personal brand is what people say about you when you aren't in the room. What do you want people to say about you? How do you want hiring managers, recruiters, and company leadership to view you when opportunities arise?

Begin by understanding your strengths, values, passions, and the unique qualities that differentiate you from others. Consider what you want to be known for in your industry. Reflect on what makes you uniquely YOU. If you're having trouble with this, ask a friend for help or connect with someone who does personal branding. We've seen many people struggle with this, and sometimes all they need is a little help from someone with an "outsider's" perspective.

Below, write your top three strengths, the three values you hold in highest esteem, and three words that you want others to use to describe you. These may be the same as those from Chapter 3, or they might be strengths for which you want to be known.

_____

_____

_____

_____

_____

Personal Brand & Vision

You took the time to develop your career vision in Chapter 4. Now let's look at your personal brand. Imagine you're in that long-term role.

How do you describe yourself? How do others describe you? Take a moment to describe your personal brand vision. We will integrate this into your broader plan as you continue your journey.

_____

_____

_____

_____

_____

Brand Narrative

Melissa worked for well over a decade at one of the most iconic American fashion brands. When she was laid off in 2020, she found herself in the middle of the COVID-19 pandemic in New York City, trying to find work in an industry that had been absolutely decimated. One of the biggest surprises to her was the realization that so much of her own sense of identity and self-worth was tied to her title and to who she had worked for. With that gone, she felt adrift.

It was dusting off her dormant LinkedIn profile (opened in 2008, first post in 2020) that gave her back her voice. By reflecting on her values, her goals, and how she wanted to be seen, Melissa crafted her brand narrative and began to share her thought leadership and build a community on the platform. This led to her successful career pivot and a whole new sense of self; one that she is enormously proud of.

She had to do the work to determine her unique value proposition, her brand, and the story she wanted to tell. There is light at the end of the tunnel when your career seems to be hitting a speed bump or taking a detour.

The goal here is to share a compelling narrative that reflects your professional journey, achievements, and challenges you've overcome. Your story should resonate with your target audience and always reflect your authentic self. Storytelling is at the heart of everything, and personal brand is no different.

You are telling the story of where you are and how you got to this point. In a later chapter, we'll set some goals for strengthening your brand. In the meantime, let's write your story.

It is important that your storytelling is authentic. Don't try to imitate what works for someone else. Your story is about you – not about them. Using someone else's tone or trying to mirror someone else's success is both inauthentic and exhausting.

Write a short paragraph (three-five sentences) that tells your professional story. Where did you start? What challenges have you overcome? What successes are you most proud of?

_____

_____

_____

_____

_____

8.4

If your career were a news article, what would the headline be? (Example: "Tech Innovator Revolutionizes Healthcare Accessibility"). This can be a delicate balance. Buzz words can be a turn-off. Use your judgment and read it out loud. If it sounds "icky" to you, change it.

_____

_____

_____

_____

_____

8.5

How do you want your brand to contribute to your field or industry? What legacy do you want to leave?

_____

_____

_____

_____

_____

Assess Your Online Presence

An online presence is critical for two reasons. Building credibility in the cyber world requires locations where you can interact with others. When you're building credibility in real life (IRL), you need a way to follow up with individuals or connect with them between interactions.

Additionally, a 2020 survey found that 79% of businesses have rejected a candidate based on their social media profiles[vi]. A separate study found that 54% of employers have eliminated a candidate based on their social media.[vii] Regardless of the study you prefer to read, there is a great chance that employers are looking at your social media to get an impression of who you are. Make sure it's a good one.

How do you show up online? Do you have a business-relevant social media presence? Do you have a professional website? Do you have a complete LinkedIn profile? Note some areas where you could improve:

_____

_____

_____

_____

_____

> **Pro Tip: Your personal brand is likely to evolve over time as you do. However, your core values should always remain the main driver of that brand.*

Thought Leadership

The transition from being a leader to a thought leader is a meaningful shift because it represents a move from achieving operational excellence to making a larger impact. As a leader, you guide your team or organization toward specific goals by managing resources and directing activities to achieve tangible results. As a thought leader, you extend your influence beyond immediate organizational boundaries through the power of ideas, innovation, and insights. You can shape industry trends, influence public opinion, and inspire change on a larger scale.

Becoming a thought leader is crucial in today's rapidly changing business environment. Your ideas and ability to inspire are just as important as your managerial expertise. By establishing yourself as a thought leader, you not only gain a competitive edge but also contribute to the broader conversation in your field, promoting innovation and strategic thinking. This move can help you build stronger connections with stakeholders, attract top talent, and create new opportunities for growth and collaboration.

Personal Branding and Thought Leadership

Personal branding is the foundation of thought leadership. It is crucial not to underestimate the significance of authenticity and integrity in your personal branding. These qualities will give you credibility as a thought leader in your industry.

Establishing expertise is essential for a thought leader. It showcases the credibility upon which your audience trusts your insights and opinions.

What is Expertise?

Expertise has three major components:

Knowledge - This is the cornerstone of expertise. It involves having a deep understanding of your field that goes beyond surface-level information. Experts have a strong foundation in their specialty's basic principles and advanced concepts. They are often well-versed in the latest research, trends, and methodologies. An expert's key traits are continuous learning and staying updated with new developments.

Experience - When it comes to claiming expertise, it's not enough to simply have knowledge. Practical experience is essential for applying that knowledge effectively. This means having a proven track record of working within the field, overcoming challenges, and using that experience to refine and improve practices. Experience enables an expert to offer insights that have been tested and proven in real-world scenarios, not just in theory.

Recognition by Others - Expertise is usually confirmed by acknowledgment from peers and other industry stakeholders. This can manifest through awards, certifications, speaking engagements at conferences, publications in reputable journals, and endorsements from other respected figures in the field. Recognition is significant as it demonstrates a widely held belief that an individual has provided valuable insights and solutions that are respected and utilized by others.

In what areas would you like to strengthen your expertise?

_____

_____

_____

_____

_____

Many times, we find leaders have strong knowledge and experience but lack recognition. Here are a few ways you can increase recognition of your field of expertise:

- **Publishing Articles** - Writing and submitting articles to popular and respected journals and industry sites.
- **Speaking Engagements** - Sharing knowledge through talks or panel discussions at industry events.
- **Online Forums and Discussions** - Actively engaging in online forums, webinars, and discussion groups.
- **Recognition by Peers** - Acknowledgment from respected peers within a field acts as a seal of approval, signaling to others that the thought leader's ideas are credible and worthy of attention. This validation can open doors to new audiences who trust the opinions of established figures or institutions.

In which areas would you benefit most from strengthening your recognition? Speaking Engagements? Publishing papers or articles?

_____

_____

_____

_____

_____

**Pro Tip: Consider refraining from labelling yourself as an expert. Demonstrating your expertise while remaining humble and showing you're in a constant state of learning is likely to be more effective. People like to follow others with confidence, not arrogance.*

"We all need people who will give us feedback.
That's how we improve."
– Bill Gates

9

Feedback

Getting feedback is a must for professional growth in today's fast-paced work environment. Especially if you're aiming for higher positions in your company, receiving constructive feedback on your performance and leadership abilities is essential. This chapter discusses why constructive feedback is crucial for your career and offers tips on using it efficiently to improve your skills and prepare for more advanced responsibilities.

Why is Feedback Important?

Continuous improvement is essential to improving your job performance and increasing your potential. Feedback is a great tool for understanding your strengths and weaknesses, thereby allowing you to work on them. By knowing what works and what does not, you can make changes and improve your job performance.

Getting feedback from others is like looking at yourself in a mirror. It gives you an insight into how others perceive your actions and leadership style. This helps you understand how your behavior affects your team and organization, which is vital for being a great leader.

Handling feedback effectively is a crucial skill for any leader. It is essential to *be open to constructive criticism and not take it personally*. Instead, leaders can use feedback to learn and grow, making them more resilient and adaptable to any challenges that may come their way.

Finally, it strengthens relationships and builds trust. Being open to feedback is a sign of humility and a desire to grow. When you actively seek feedback, you create trust and build better relationships with your colleagues. This helps create a culture of continuous improvement and respect.

We've been in many situations where we've asked for feedback and not received it. Our recommendations here come from years of trial and error. Simply asking, "Do you have any feedback for me?" often fails. For a number of reasons, people are unable or unwilling to give feedback when asked this question. Here are our strategies for increasing the likelihood that you'll actually receive the feedback.

How to Ask for Feedback

It's strategic for your career growth to actively seek feedback instead of waiting for it to come to you. So, why not ask your supervisor, peers, and direct reports for feedback regularly? You should be specific about the areas you need input in and show your appreciation for their insights.

Choose an appropriate time and a comfortable setting for both of you. Avoid asking for feedback when the person is obviously busy or stressed. Express your appreciation for their time and willingness to provide insight. Let them know specifically that you value their opinion and want to improve.

Instead of asking vague questions like "Do you have any feedback?", focus on particular areas: "I'm working on improving my presentation skills; could you give me feedback on my clarity and delivery?" or "Could you share your thoughts on how I handled that challenging client interaction?" This makes the feedback more actionable for you and easier for them to give.

 9.1

Here are a few questions to get you started:
- From whom will you first seek feedback?
- What specific feedback will you seek?
- When will you ask for that feedback?

Consider asking for feedback on your skills, network, and brand.

_____

_____

_____

_____

_____

How you receive the feedback is critical to getting feedback in the future. Focus on understanding the perspective of the person giving feedback instead of getting defensive. If something is unclear, ask, "Could you give me a specific example of what you mean?" This shows you're engaged and want to use their feedback effectively. Take notes to reference later.

Express genuine thanks for their time and honesty. Let them know that you will consider their input carefully as you work towards improvement. This fosters positive relationships and makes that person more open to giving you feedback in the future.

After the feedback session, take some time to reflect on what you've heard. Consider the feedback from multiple perspectives and identify the core areas that need improvement.

As you receive feedback, you can document it here. This will help you in setting goals for attaining skills and experience in the future.

_____

_____

_____

_____

_____

> **Pro Tip: Don't forget to update those who gave you feedback on your efforts and progress. This shows that you're committed to growing personally and encourages ongoing communication, strengthening your relationships. Sharing what you've learned and how you've improved can also motivate others to seek and use feedback actively.*

Make sure you include this feedback in your skill, network, and brand gaps and goals. You can also include those you asked for feedback in your **stakeholder tracking spreadsheet** so you can follow up on your progress!

https://is.gd/stakeholdertracking

III. Goal... Plan... Execute!

Your career isn't a game of chance; it's a strategic chess match where you control the pieces.

Section three is your guide to mastering the board. We'll help you identify your most valuable pieces, plot your path to victory, and develop the skills to outmaneuver any challenges.

This section will empower you to make calculated moves and create a winning game plan for your career.

> "Setting goals is the first step in turning the invisible into the visible."
> – Tony Robbins

10

Goals

Now that you've done the foundational work, it's time to set some goals to help you move forward.

Remember Your Vision

In Chapter 4, you set a vision for your career.

Achieving your vision requires a series of goals. We'll set longer-term goals and then shorter-term goals. Combined, these will significantly increase the probability of you achieving your vision.

Long-Term Career Goal

These long-term goals can be somewhat generic, but you'll want enough detail to guide your shorter-term goals. You don't want to create a goal that significantly limits your options.

Cindy has coached many leaders who have a very specific role in mind. Often, that specific role is at a specific company. This really narrows the opportunity for these individuals to achieve their goal. Not that they aren't capable, but that there are probably a number of individuals who seek out that role. And while we all think we're too valuable to be impacted by a restructuring at a company, in truth, no one is too valuable. As a leader, you intentionally have to build a team that can be successful without you. So this is one area that is important for you to think big to build in options and resilience.

Pro Tip: Take this exercise seriously. Don't limit yourself to a single option. This is where most people go wrong. Be different!

Role

Describe the type of work you're doing, the people you're working with, the size of the team, etc. You might consider including some titles that are appropriate, but don't limit yourself to one. That narrows your options and decreases your chances for success.

_____

_____

_____

_____

_____

Skills

What skills might you need for this role? What skills are you missing? These might be executive presence, strategic decision-making, etc.

_____

_____

_____

_____

_____

Network

What network might you need for this role? Are there people with specific titles with which you'll need to be connected to be recommended for the role?

_____

_____

_____

_____

_____

Brand Goals

Is your brand where you want it to be for that future role? Odds are that you still need to work on it or even evolve it as you progress through your career. Let's build some goals around your brand.

Choose one aspect of your brand you want to strengthen. Is it your expertise in a particular skill? Your reputation in a specific industry? Your thought leadership on a certain topic?

_____

_____

_____

_____

_____

Repeat the process, focusing on a different aspect of your brand.

_____

_____

_____

_____

_____

Career Two–Five-Year Goals

This is far more specific. It is a list of possible roles that might get you to your five-to ten-year goals. These are the roles that will build the skills and network described above.

As you set goals that are closer in time, it's important that those goals be SMART goals: Specific, Measurable, Achievable, Relevant, and Time-bound. For instance, rather than vaguely aiming to "improve leadership skills," set a goal to "lead a project team successfully within the next six months by completing a leadership training course and applying new strategies." This method transforms abstract aspirations into actionable, concrete goals.

Thought Leadership Goals

Thought leadership is not just about self-promotion; it's about offering valuable perspectives, challenging conventional wisdom, and inspiring others. It's about positioning yourself as a trusted authority and a go-to resource in your field.

In what areas could you develop thought leadership? Share ideas below:

_____

_____

_____

_____

_____

It's helpful to have your values and goals all in one location. You can use the next page, or you can download the notebook here.

https://is.gd/9dYfPY	https://is.gd/JkP6Qa
Printable PDF	**Fillable PDF**

Values	Career Vision
_____	_____
_____	_____
_____	5-10 Year Career Goals
_____	_____
_____	_____

Skill Goals	Network Goals
_____	_____
_____	_____
_____	_____
_____	_____

Brand Goals	Thought Leadership Goals
_____	_____
_____	_____
_____	_____

"The journey of a thousand miles begins with a single step."
– Lao Tzu

11

Build Your Plan

You know your goals, skills, network, brand, and gaps. It's time to build your plan for the next few years.

Career Plan

Now you're playing chess. If you don't know how to play chess, that's not a problem. Cindy plays chess, but not well. She can only see about two moves ahead on a really good day. So we're sticking with looking two moves ahead.

The gist is that you're going to run a few scenarios. Your five-ten-year objective likely requires one or two intermediate moves. In this game, you want to visualize a move and then the potential outcomes from that move. Where can you go from that position? What skills and network will you gain? Remember, titles may vary from organization to organization. Keep this in mind as you build your plan.

We'll start with a blank plan. You can fill this out in the book or use the PDF, which is available for download.

Start with the top boxes. Write the roles you identified in Chapter 10 for your five-to-ten-year goals. What skills and network might you need to get those roles or to be successful in those roles? Now move to the bottom row. What skills do you have? What network do you have?

What steps might you take to get to those roles in the top row? These go in the middle. Use the information from Chapter 10 for your two to five-year goals. Put the roles, skills, network, and any brand elements needed and gained here.

Finally, we'll move to the lateral role on the bottom right of this plan.

Lateral Moves

Switching to a different department or function at the same level can be super helpful for leaders looking to broaden their skill sets, make new connections, and open up better career prospects in the future.

Sideways moves help leaders gain diverse experiences, understand different aspects of the business, and develop a more comprehensive view of the company. This can push leaders out of their comfort zone, help them tackle new problems, and learn different strategies, which is crucial for personal and professional growth.

By moving laterally, leaders can broaden their skill sets by exposing themselves to different challenges, workflows, and team dynamics. This diversity fosters versatility and adaptability, which are highly valued qualities in senior leadership roles.

Additionally, experiencing different functions provides a comprehensive understanding of the business. Leaders can gain insights into how various departments contribute to overall goals, enhancing their ability to make informed decisions.

Sound a little complicated? Never fear. We have an example for you.

Example Career Plan

2nd Step - 5-10 Years

VP, Product Marketing	Sr. Dir / VP Strategy	VP Sales Engineering

Skills / Network

Need:

	VP, Product Marketing		Sr. Dir / VP Strategy		VP Sales Engineering	
Skills:	Network:	Skills:	Network:	Skills:	Network:
Large Team	VP Marketing	Operational Experience	SVP Sales	Large Team	VP Sales
Geographic Coverage	VP Sales	Executive Presence	VP Pr. Mkt	Geographic Coverage	SVP Sales Eng.
Executive Presence	VP of Eng.	Strategic Planning	VP Finance	Executive Presence	VP Product Mktg.
Technical Breadth				Technical Breadth	

Gained:

Skills:	Network:	Skills:	Network:	Skills:	Network:
Multiple Tech.	SVP Marketing	Large Scale Bus. Strat.	SVP Pr. Mkt	Multiple Technologies	SVP Sales
P&L Experience	SVP Sales	C-Suite Presence	SVP Operations	Global Experience	SVP Operations
	SVP of Engineering	P&L	SVP Finance		SVP Pr. Mkt.

Next Step - 2-5 Years

Dir/Sr. Manager Product Marketing	Chief of Staff	Dir/Sr. Manager Sales Engineering

Skills / Network

Need:

Skills:	Network:	Skills:	Network:	Skills:	Network:
Bigger Picture Persp.	Dir Marketing	Strategic Thinking	Relevant VPs	Bigger Picture Persp.	Dir Sales
Cross-fxn Lead.	Dir Eng.	Cross-fxn Lead.	Dir. Strategy & Plan.	Cross-fxn Lead.	Dir Sales Eng.
Technical Breadth		Operational Exp.		Technical Breadth	

Gained:

Skills	Network:	Skills:	Network:	Skills:	Network:
Manage Managers	VP Marketing	Budget Management	Relevant VP & SVP	Manage Managers	VP Sales
Budget Management	VP Engineering	Deep Operations Know.	Operations Leadership	Budget Management	VP Engineering
		Leading w. Influence			

Current Position / Lateral Move

Manager, Product Marketing		Manager, Product Marketing Different Product

Skills / Network

Gained:

Skills:	Network:		Skills:	Network:
Team Management	Dir Marketing	Gained:	Team Management	Dir Marketing Multiple Prod.
Product Management	Dir Engineering		Broader Product Exp.	Dir Eng. Multiple Prod.
Customer Service	Dir. Sales		Broader Customer Know.	Multiple Sales Leaders

Pro Tip: Most people focus on a single role or title, which is truly limiting. Think about each level of an organization. The number of roles decreases significantly with each level you rise in an organization. Give yourself options to maximize your potential for success.

STAND-OUT PERSONAL BRAND

It's your turn. Use the sheet below to plan your career strategy.

2nd Step - 5-10 Years

| Skills / Network | Skills / Network | Skills / Network |

Need:

Gained:

Next Step - 2-5 Years

| Skills / Network | Skills / Network | Skills / Network |

Need:

Gained:

Current Position — Skills / Network — **Gained:**

Lateral Move — Skills / Network

"Anyone who stops learning is old, whether at twenty or eighty. Anyone who keeps learning stays young."
– Henry Ford

12

Expanding Your Skillset

The first key to a successful future is coming to terms with the idea that you'll be learning forever. But never fear, if you don't currently identify as a lifelong learner, there are many ways to become one that will suit your personality and lifestyle.

Leaders who are eager to learn new things are better equipped to lead teams, make their organizations more successful, and adapt to changes in their business environment. Proactively developing new skills enhances leadership abilities and can help attract the attention of higher-ups, opening new opportunities for promotion and leadership roles.

We are both lifelong learners. This is a significant advantage for both of us. We find many ways to incorporate learning into our daily and weekly routines. Simply focusing on continuous learning will give you a competitive advantage. Here are a few things to keep in mind:

Identify High-Demand Skills

In what areas do you see the highest growth for your organization? Is it cybersecurity? Artificial intelligence? Find these areas where you see investment either in your organization or in your industry. These are areas that are worth your investment of time in learning. As you learn, share the resources that you find valuable. Part of your value to a team or organization is in what you share with others to make them better. This is part of being a great teammate and leader.

Collaborating with Other Teams

Seek opportunities to work on projects with teams from different departments. This exposure can provide insights into various aspects of the business and help you develop a more holistic understanding of your organization. Which departments would you enjoy working with using the passions you identified in the previous chapters? Reach out to leaders or peers in those departments. What are their biggest challenges? How might you help them solve those challenges? Will you learn something that will contribute to your building and enhancing your own unique value or skills?

What team projects could you propose or participate in?

_____

_____

_____

_____

_____

Courses and Communities

Commit to lifelong learning by taking courses, attending workshops, and pursuing certifications relevant to your industry and beyond. Online platforms like Coursera, LinkedIn Learning, and Udemy offer various courses catering to different interests and professional needs.

Check out the Valiant Leadership Community! In this community, we have weekly group coaching and continuous learning opportunities designed to help busy leaders accelerate their leadership careers.

This community, led by Dr. Cindy Goodwin-Sak, is a safe place to discuss current leadership topics, learn new skills, and expand your network. Get a 20% discount using this link:

https://is.gd/valiantbookinsider

With the QR code below, you can get a free one-week trial in the DIY Influence Community. This supportive community is the place to go for guidance on all things personal branding, thought leadership, and figuring out what might come next in your career. We spoke earlier about how entrepreneurship and consulting are rewarding career options that both come with risk. The DIY Influence community will help you develop your voice, find and serve your audience, and build your business. What's even more exciting, you can connect directly with and learn from Melissa Cohen, one of the community founders.

https://diyinfluence.com/

If being part of a community isn't for you, DIY Influence offers a four-week intensive Personal Brand Bootcamp (which includes one month of access to everything that the community offers). For information specific to the bootcamp, visit **www.diyinfluence.com/bootcamp**

What courses or communities would be beneficial?

_____

_____

_____

_____

Books & Podcasts

Books and podcasts offer you, as a leader, an accessible and flexible way to continuously expand your knowledge and sharpen your abilities. Books provide in-depth explorations of leadership principles, strategies, and case studies from successful figures. They allow you to dive into complex subjects and reflect on your own practices. Podcasts, on the other hand, offer bite- sized insights, interviews with thought leaders, and discussions on the latest trends within the business landscape. These easily digestible formats can be integrated into your busy schedule for on-the-go learning.

Through targeted exposure to diverse perspectives and new ideas, both books and podcasts serve as catalysts for your growth. They can challenge your assumptions, offer solutions to current problems, and spark innovation for the future. By staying engaged with the wealth of knowledge available through books and podcasts, you demonstrate a commitment to continuous development, ultimately benefiting not only yourself but your entire team and organization.

Some of our favorites are:

Books:

1. Five Dysfunctions of a Team - Patrick Lencioni
2. Speed of Trust - Stephen M. R. Covey
3. Dare to Lead - Brené Brown

Podcasts

1. WorkLife with Adam Grant
2. Career Blast in A Half - Loren Greiff
3. Heartbeat for Hire - Lyndsay Dowd

There are so many that we had to restrain our recommendations significantly. These are a few that are truly great.

What books or podcasts can you consume to continue building your skillset?

_____

_____

_____

_____

_____

Self and Team Assessments

You learned about seeking feedback in Chapter 8. Now let's look at some other tools that can provide you a unique view of your skills. Some tools we recommend are:

Self-Assessments

DISC - https://www.truity.com/test/disc-personality-test
Strengths Finder (CliftonStrengths) - https://is.gd/VpP8Tq
Emotional Intelligence - https://is.gd/l1w05A
VL Assessment –https://is.gd/assessself

Team Assessments

VL Assessment Team – https://is.gd/teamassess

✏️ 12.4

What assessments will you try?

_____

_____

_____

_____

Stretch Assignments

Stretch assignments are tasks or projects that go beyond your current role's scope and responsibilities. They require you to step out of your comfort zone, learn new skills, and tackle unfamiliar challenges. The beauty of stretch assignments lies in their dual benefit: they contribute to personal and professional growth while simultaneously showcasing your capabilities to the organization.

Leadership is not confined to title or position. It is demonstrated through actions—particularly in how one handles challenges. By taking on stretch assignments, you exhibit several critical leadership qualities:

- **Initiative** - Volunteering for additional tasks shows a readiness to take on new challenges without being asked.
- **Adaptability** - Successfully navigating unfamiliar terrain proves your ability to adapt to new situations and learn quickly.
- **Problem-solving** - Stretch assignments often come with unforeseen obstacles, offering you a platform to demonstrate your problem-solving skills.
- **Teamwork and Collaboration** - These projects frequently require cross- departmental collaboration, showcasing your ability to lead and work effectively with diverse teams.
-

Stretch assignments can significantly increase your visibility within the organization. By contributing to projects outside your usual remit, you interact with a broader range of colleagues, including senior leadership. This exposure is invaluable; it allows key decision-makers to witness your skills, work ethic, and potential firsthand, leading to greater recognition and opportunities for advancement.

Here are a few key things to remember about stretch assignments:

1. **Be Proactive** - Don't wait for opportunities to come to you. Seek out stretch assignments and special projects that align with your career goals and the company's objectives.

2. **Communicate Effectively** - Keep stakeholders updated on your progress and the project's outcomes. Effective communication is key to ensuring your efforts are recognized.
3. **Seek Feedback** - Regularly ask for feedback on your performance. This demonstrates your commitment to improvement and helps identify areas for development.
4. **Reflect and Learn** - After completing a project, take the time to reflect on what you learned and how it applies to your career development.
5. **Document Your Achievements** - Keep a record of the projects you've worked on, the skills you've developed, and the outcomes achieved. This will be invaluable during performance reviews or discussions about career advancement.

Taking on stretch assignments and special projects is a proactive way to develop and demonstrate your leadership skills and dedication. These opportunities allow you to contribute significantly to your organization while enhancing your visibility and positioning yourself for recognition and promotion. Embrace these challenges with enthusiasm and an open mind, and you'll set yourself apart as a valuable asset to your company and a strong candidate for leadership roles.

What stretch assignments could you take on?

___

*Pro Tip: Download podcasts, audiobooks, anything that helps you grow. Listen while you're exercising, doing housework, or other tasks that might not require your full attention. Or, put learning on your calendar. The excuse of "I'm too busy" is just poor prioritization.

> "Leadership is not about being in charge. It is about taking care of those in your charge."
> – Simon Sinek

13

Power Skills

Being technically proficient is not enough to succeed in leadership. In fact, being too focused on technical skills likely will hinder your success as a leader. Soft skills such as emotional intelligence, communication, and negotiation are crucial for shaping effective leaders who can inspire their teams, drive change, and create a positive work environment. This chapter explores how improving these soft skills can open up new leadership opportunities and help you grow professionally.

Why Do We Call Them Soft Skills?

The term soft skills is in no way meant to undermine or decrease the importance of skills such as emotional intelligence and communication. This phrase comes from the US military. In the 1960s and 1970s, the US military determined they were very good at training soldiers on skills requiring physical machinery or hard objects such as equipment and weapons. However, they hadn't developed training for skills that don't involve tangible items. They simply lumped all such skills into the phrase 'soft skills'. This isn't a commentary on that decision. It's simply how the phrase was coined.

However, as society and technology evolve, these skills have become incredibly critical to the success of leaders. In fact, these skills are some of the most powerful in a leader's toolbox.

Let's flip the script and call them power skills.

While the phrase "power skills" has been attributed to several individuals and organizations, Lyndsay Dowd first brought it to the authors' attention. She has been instrumental in the evolution of many leaders' journeys.

What are Power Skills?

Power skills that are truly impactful for a leader generally fall into one of three categories: communication, interpersonal skills, and cognitive/self-management skills. These skills can be incredibly difficult to learn, but with continuous effort and self-reflection, you can build these skills like any others. Let's dive a little deeper.

Communication

Executive communication skills are a special set of abilities tailored for top leaders. They go beyond basic interpersonal skills and require a strategic approach to convey complex information, inspire action, and build trust among diverse stakeholders.

Effective executive communication is all about being clear, concise, confident, and impactful. It means simplifying complex ideas into simple messages that resonate with everyone in the organization. Executives need to present information that aligns with the company's vision and values while also being open and authentic.

Telling stories strategically is a big part of executive communication. Leaders must be able to tell stories that connect with employees, investors, and customers on an emotional level, creating a sense of shared purpose and excitement for the future. This involves creating engaging presentations, speeches, and written communications that capture attention and leave a lasting impression.

Executive communication also means being able to adapt to different audiences and situations. Whether it's speaking at a board meeting, leading a town hall, or engaging with the media, executives need to tailor their message and delivery to fit the specific audience and purpose. This means understanding the needs and interests of different stakeholders, anticipating potential concerns, and delivering information in a way that fosters understanding and support.

Executive communication skills are more crucial than ever. Leaders who can master these skills will be well-prepared to tackle complex challenges, inspire their teams, and drive their organizations toward success.

What communication skills may you want to develop?

___

___

___

___

___

Interpersonal Skills

Interpersonal skills are crucial for effective leadership, especially for senior leaders and executives who handle complex relationships and drive organizational success. These skills go beyond just talking and cover a wider range of abilities that build trust, collaboration, and influence.

Emotional intelligence is at the heart of interpersonal leadership. Executives need to be in touch with their own emotions and understand how they affect others. They should also be able to see things from others' perspectives, creating a more inclusive and supportive environment. Additionally, skilled leaders excel at managing relationships, connecting with diverse stakeholders, and handling conflicts with grace and diplomacy.

Building trust is another key interpersonal skill. Leaders who show integrity, honesty, and transparency earn the respect and loyalty of their teams. This creates a culture of psychological safety where employees feel comfortable sharing ideas, taking risks, and speaking up when they have concerns. This trust encourages open communication, collaboration, and innovation, ultimately driving better outcomes for the organization.

Influence and persuasion are essential for executives who need to rally support for their vision and initiatives. This involves not only making strong arguments but also understanding the motivations and concerns of different stakeholders. Leaders who can connect with others on a personal level, build coalitions, and negotiate effectively are more likely to gain buy-in and achieve their goals.

By honing these skills, leaders can create a positive and productive work environment, build strong relationships with stakeholders, and drive sustainable success for their organizations.

What interpersonal skills could you continue to develop?

_____

_____

_____

_____

_____

Now, document these in your skill gaps list in Chapter 6 or here on your overall plan.

Cognitive / Self-Management Skills

Cognitive and self-management skills are the mental tools that empower senior leaders and executives to navigate complex challenges, make sound decisions, and drive organizational success. These skills are the foundation of effective leadership, enabling executives to think strategically, manage their emotions, and adapt to changing circumstances.

Critical thinking and problem-solving are essential cognitive skills for executives. They must be able to analyze information, identify patterns, and evaluate potential solutions. This involves asking probing questions, challenging assumptions, and considering diverse perspectives. Strong problem-solving skills enable leaders to address challenges head-on, make informed decisions, and implement effective solutions.

Strategic thinking is another crucial cognitive skill. Executives must be able to see the big picture, anticipate future trends, and develop long-term strategies. This involves understanding the competitive landscape, identifying opportunities and threats, and aligning resources to achieve organizational goals. Strategic thinkers are able to make decisions that not only address immediate needs but also position the organization for future success.

Self-management skills are equally important for senior leaders and executives. Emotional regulation is key, as leaders must be able to manage their own emotions in high-pressure situations. This involves maintaining composure, avoiding impulsive reactions, and responding to challenges in a calm and rational manner. Self-awareness is also crucial, as leaders must understand their own strengths, weaknesses, and biases. This self-knowledge enables them to make better decisions, delegate effectively, and seek feedback and development opportunities.

Executives who master these skills will be well-positioned to lead their organizations through uncertainty, adapt to new challenges, and achieve sustainable success.

 13.3

What cognitive and self-management skills do you wish to build?

_____

_____

_____

_____

_____

> **Pro Tip: These skills are a life-long journey. Don't be hard on yourself if you find yourself responding or communicating instinctively rather than thoughtfully. You are human, after all.*

"If you cannot see where you are going, ask someone who has been there before."
– J. Loren Norris

14

Mentors & Sponsors

Having a mentor can be a game-changer for leaders. An experienced mentor can guide you and bring a new perspective to help you navigate your career.

Mentors can give you insights and knowledge to help you avoid mistakes, make informed decisions, and learn from their experience. This helps you learn faster. A mentor can also introduce you to other professionals, leading to opportunities for collaboration, visibility, and advancement. A bigger network means more access to opportunity!

With a mentor's support and feedback, you'll feel more confident in your abilities and decisions, allowing you to take on new challenges.

Finding a Mentor

Finding a mentor is relatively easy. If you know who you would like to have mentor you, there are a couple of ways to ask.

The Indirect Approach

Start with seeking advice. Rather than asking outright for mentorship, ask for their advice on a specific challenge or goal. This is a lower-pressure way to build a relationship. Then, demonstrate value. Take initiative, be proactive with follow-up, and show a genuine dedication to learning. This makes a mentee more attractive to potential mentors.

The Direct Approach

Simply reaching out and asking is also an option. Here are a couple of ideas on how you might phrase an ask like that:

> *"I admire your work in [field/industry] and am inspired by your career path. Would you be open to a brief informational meeting to discuss your experiences and how I might navigate my own journey?"*

> *"I'm seeking guidance in [specific area of interest] and believe your expertise would be invaluable. Would you consider mentoring me, perhaps meeting monthly to discuss my goals and challenges?"*

In this case, being direct means seeking to understand directly with the potential mentor what value exchange might be possible. When being direct, we recommend avoiding the question, "Will you be my mentor?" That question lacks details such as topic, time investment, and value to the potential mentor. Melissa and Cindy have both gotten this question. It's awkward and creates a lot of angst as we try to figure out what might be expected of us.

The Network Approach

> *Pro Tip: Demonstrate value. For someone to give you their time they need to find value in that experience. Don't just assume they enjoy spending time with you. Find articles to share based on their interests, ask about the challenges they face, and seek informed, creative perspectives to share. Add value to your mentor or anyone with whom you want to build a network.*

Tap into your existing network. Reach out to your current or former managers or colleagues you respect, potentially even former professors. Let them know you're seeking mentorship and why you value their perspective. Again, like the direct approach, don't simply ask them to mentor you. Give context, specific topics that interest you, and suggested time frames. You can also ask for their recommendations for other experts and an introduction.

Who will you ask about mentorship, and on what topics?

_____

_____

_____

_____

_____

The Benefits of Becoming a Mentor

While seeking mentors is invaluable, the act of becoming a mentor also significantly contributes to your leadership development:

1. Teaching and guiding others allows you to refine your leadership style, improve your communication, and develop empathy.
2. Engaging with mentees can introduce fresh ideas and perspectives to your own thinking, preventing stagnation and promoting innovation.
3. Mentoring allows you to leave a lasting impact on your industry by shaping the leaders of tomorrow and contributing to a legacy that transcends your immediate work.

Being a mentor can elevate your standing within your organization and industry, as it showcases your commitment to growth and development. It's also a great thing to add to your resume to demonstrate your commitment to growing others.

> **Pro Tip: Check with your organization or university to see if they have a mentorship program. These programs are common, but often not well-advertised.*

Who might you consider mentoring?

_____

_____

_____

_____

_____

Strategies for Effective Mentorship

To get the most out of mentorship, whether you're looking for a mentor or you're the one doing the mentoring, here are some tips to keep in mind:

1. **Be Clear About What You Want -** Whether you're the mentor or the mentee, it's important to know what you want to achieve from the relationship.
2. **Consistency is Key -** Mentorship takes time and effort. Make sure you stay in touch regularly and communicate openly to keep the momentum going.
3. **Set a Timeline –** As mentorship is focused, ensure that you set an estimated time frame for mentoring. This is beneficial to both the mentor and mentee.
4. **Respect and Honesty -** Trust, respect, and honesty are important for a strong mentor-mentee relationship. Be open to feedback and be willing to talk about both successes and failures.
5. **Listen Carefully and Engage -** Whether you're giving or receiving advice, it's important to listen carefully. Be fully present, ask questions, and show genuine interest.
6. **Track Your Progress -** Set some goals for your mentorship and check in periodically to see how you're doing. This will help keep you focused and make sure you're making progress.

Mentorship is a great way to develop your leadership skills and advance your career. If you can find a mentor, you can get valuable guidance and insights. And if you become a mentor, you can help someone else grow and develop. In today's world, mentorship can lead to new opportunities, relationships, and levels of success.

Sponsors

While having a mentor is incredibly helpful in building your skills and accelerating your career, having a sponsor is truly game-changing.

Mentors are primarily focused on providing guidance, advice, and support. They share their knowledge, experience, and insights to help you grow professionally and personally. They offer career advice, share industry knowledge, help you develop skills, provide feedback and encouragement, and act as a sounding board.

While mentors talk with you, sponsors talk about you. They actively advocate for your advancement within the organization. They use their influence, connections, and power to create opportunities and open doors. Sponsors promote your work and accomplishments, advocate for you in important meetings and discussions, introduce you to key stakeholders, and create opportunities for you to showcase your abilities.

Mentorship is a more accessible form of support. Finding a sponsor can be more challenging as it requires more trust and commitment from the sponsor. You may even have a sponsor without knowing it. That was our experience. We often had people sharing our work and recommending us for various positions. But it's incredibly helpful to know that someone is sponsoring you so that you can influence the conversations in which they're representing you.

Asking someone to be your sponsor can be a delicate conversation. Cindy has had several people email or jump on a one-on-one meeting, not having previously met, and asked her, "Will you be my sponsor?" When we discuss the direct approach below, that's not it. Before asking for sponsorship, you need well-established trust. That might come through mentorship or through working together on projects. If you've built trust with someone, here are a few approaches you can take, depending on the nature of your relationship and the context:

The Direct Approach

If you already have a strong relationship with the person and believe they have a vested interest in your success, you can be more direct:

Example: "I'm really excited about [specific goal or opportunity]. I know you have a lot of experience and influence in this area. Would you be willing to be my sponsor and help me achieve this?"

The Indirect Approach

If you're less certain of their willingness or want to gauge their interest first, you can approach the topic indirectly:

Example: "I've been thinking about [specific goal or opportunity] and would love to get your insights. Would you be open to discussing how I could best position myself for success?"

During this conversation, you can share your aspirations and seek their advice. If they seem supportive and offer to help, you can then broach the topic of sponsorship more explicitly. Highlight how their sponsorship could benefit both of you. Explain how their involvement could enhance their reputation, strengthen their network, or contribute to their legacy.

Regardless of their response, express your gratitude for their time and consideration. If they decline, thank them for their honesty and ask if they would be willing to offer any other forms of support or guidance.

For either approach, here are a few tips:

- **Do your research** - Before approaching a potential sponsor, research their background, interests, and areas of expertise. This will help you tailor your request and demonstrate your understanding of their value.
- **Be prepared** - Have a clear and concise plan for how you envision their sponsorship. Outline your goals, the steps you plan to take, and how their support could make a difference.
- **Be genuine** - Express your sincere admiration for their achievements and explain why you believe their sponsorship would be invaluable.
- **Be patient** - Don't expect an immediate answer. Give them time to consider your request and weigh their options.

Asking for sponsorship is about building a mutually beneficial relationship. By demonstrating your value, potential, and appreciation for their support, you increase your chances of finding a sponsor who is truly invested in your success.

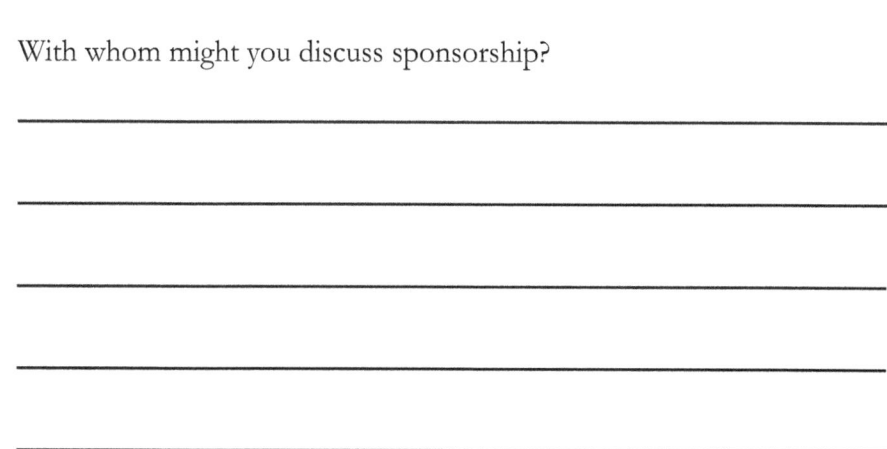

With whom might you discuss sponsorship?

_____

_____

_____

_____

"Thought leadership is not about being known. It's about being known for making a difference."
– Maria Pinelli

15

Thought Leadership Content

Creating compelling content that reflects your expertise and vision is essential to establish credibility and become known as a thought leader. It is ideal to determine your content pillars ahead of time so that you have a strategy and a game plan for your content. This does not mean that you can never deviate from these topics, but in order to establish yourself as a thought leader, you will need to have consistency. Create a simple template that outlines your content pillars (aim for three-five) and the key messages for each.

Here is an example:

Pillar	Description	Key Messages
Industry Insights	Deep dives into current events, innovations, and challenges within the industry.	Analysis of recent industry breakthroughs. Impacts of global economic changes on the industry. Emerging challenges and how to tackle them.
Leadership Lessons	Sharing knowledge and experiences related to effective leadership and management.	Key traits of successful leaders in the digital era. Strategies for fostering team creativity and innovation. Lessons learned from leadership challenges.
Industry Trends	Exploring the latest trends shaping the industry and predictions for the future.	Technological advancements driving the industry forward. Shifts in consumer behavior and market demands. Predictions for the industry in the next decade.
Success Stories/Spotlight Posts	Highlighting significant achievements within the industry or profiling notable individuals and organizations.	Inspirational stories of innovation and success. Spotlight on emerging leaders and their contributions. Case studies of successful projects and their impact.
Personal Interest Stories	Sharing personal experiences, hobbies, or interests to provide a more human aspect to the professional persona.	How personal hobbies contribute to professional skills. Stories from travels or cultural experiences. Lessons from personal challenges and their application in professional life.

Create your own content plan or use ours!

https://is.gd/thoughtleadership

Engagement Strategies

Engagement strategies and follow-up actions for your content are critical. It's the interaction with others that truly builds connection and recognition of your expertise. Here are some examples of how you can put strategies into place for different forms of content based on the pillars above:

Industry Insights Article

Interactive Infographic - Include an interactive infographic within the article that readers can click through to see different statistics or case studies related to your insights.

Comment Prompt - End the article with a thought-provoking question or prompt for readers to share their experiences or opinions in the comments.

Highlight Reader Contributions - Create a follow-up article or social media post highlighting the best insights or comments from readers, giving credit to their contributions.

Expert Roundup Webinar - Host a webinar with industry experts discussing the article's theme, incorporating questions and comments from your article's readers.

Leadership Lessons Video

Challenge or Call-to-Action - At the end of the video, challenge viewers to apply a specific leadership lesson within the next week and share their stories or outcomes.

Social Media Clip Sharing - Share short, impactful clips from the video on social media platforms with captions that invite discussion or reactions.

User Story Compilation - Compile and share stories or outcomes from viewers who took on the challenge, either in a follow-up video or a detailed blog post.

Interactive Q&A Session - Host a live Q&A session on a platform like LinkedIn or Instagram, inviting viewers to ask questions or share insights related to the leadership topics discussed.

Success Story Blog Post

Behind-the-Scenes Content: Share behind-the-scenes content or additional anecdotes related to the success story on social media, inviting readers to learn more by reading the full post.

Community Engagement: Encourage readers to nominate peers or colleagues who have their own success stories, promising to feature these in future posts.

Follow-Up Features: Create a series or segment on your blog or social media dedicated to community-nominated success stories, building a narrative of inspiration and collective achievement.

Interactive Discussions: Organize a virtual roundtable or discussion panel with the individuals featured in the success stories, allowing your audience to engage directly and ask questions.

Personal Interest Story

Personal Insights: Share personal insights or lessons learned from your personal interest story, inviting your audience to reflect on how these could apply to their own lives or careers.

Visual Storytelling: Utilize platforms like Instagram or Pinterest to share visual elements related to your personal interest story, using captions to tie back to the professional lessons or insights gained.

Audience Engagement Series - Start a series where your audience can submit their own stories or photos related to the theme, creating a community-driven content series.

Live Interactive Session - Host a live session on social media where you discuss the story more deeply, and invite your audience to share their thoughts or similar stories.

By employing different engagement strategies and follow-up actions, you can create an interactive environment around your content. This approach not only enhances audience engagement but also creates a sense of community and ongoing dialogue, which is crucial for establishing and maintaining thought leadership.

 **15.1**

What content pillars and engagement strategies are most compelling to you?

_____

_____

_____

_____

_____

15.2

What content pillars and engagement strategies might benefit your network and brand? These might be a bit outside your comfort zone.

_____

_____

_____

_____

_____

Leveraging Public Speaking and Media Appearances

Public speaking and media appearances are pivotal for professionals aiming to establish themselves as thought leaders in their field. These platforms offer a unique opportunity to share knowledge, influence others, and gain visibility.

Further, public speaking allows professionals to articulate their expertise and insights in front of an audience, thereby building credibility. It serves as a direct channel to influence peers, stakeholders, and potential clients. Engagements at conferences, seminars, and webinars help in networking with industry leaders and peers, facilitating a deeper connection with the professional community. This visibility is crucial for being recognized as a thought leader.

Some tips and guidelines for effective public speaking and presentation include:

- **Know Your Audience -** Tailor your content to the interests, knowledge level, and needs of your audience.
- **Clear and Concise Message -** Have a clear message. Use simple language and avoid company or industry specific jargon unless it is common among your audience.
- **Engage with Stories -** People relate to stories more than data. Use relevant anecdotes to illustrate points and make your message memorable. Remember the importance of storytelling that we covered earlier.
- **Practice and Prepare -** Familiarize yourself with your material well enough that you can focus on engaging with the audience rather than recalling your next point.
- **Visual Aids -** Use slides, videos, or infographics to support your points, but ensure they complement your speech rather than

overwhelm it.
- **Feedback and Reflect** - Seek feedback and reflect on your performance to continuously improve your skills.

Tips and guidelines for securing media appearances – and making the most of them include:

- **Develop a Strong Pitch** - Media outlets look for compelling stories or unique perspectives. Craft a pitch that highlights the relevance and timeliness of your content.
- **Target Appropriate Outlets** - Identify media outlets whose audience aligns with your target demographic. Tailor your approach based on whether these outlets are traditional media (TV, radio) or online platforms (blogs) ,media (TV, radio), or online platforms (blogs, podcasts).
- **Prepare for Different Formats** - Understand the format of the media appearance—whether it's a live interview, a panel discussion, or a guest article. Each format requires a different style of preparation.
- **Be Ready to Simplify Complex Ideas** - Simplifying complex ideas (without being too surface level) is key, especially in media. Be prepared to explain your area of expertise in a way that is accessible to a lay audience.

After your appearance, follow up with the media outlet to thank them, and share the segment on your social media to extend its reach. This can also foster relationships for future appearances.

 15.3

What public speaking venues or media might be best for your audience?

_____

_____

_____

_____

_____

Pro Tip: The best thought leadership pieces come from when you write from your unique lived experience. What is something that you have deep knowledge on, that you also feel passionately about? Expertise without feeling or vice versa will tend to fall flat.

IV. Troubleshooting

Even the best-laid plans can encounter unexpected obstacles. This section is your lifeline when things get tough.

Here, we'll tackle common challenges like office politics, setbacks, and self-doubt head-on. You'll find practical strategies to navigate these hurdles, ensuring your career journey stays on track…

… no matter what life throws your way.

> "Office politics are the unwritten rules of the game."
> - Unknown

16

Organizational Politics

In the professional world, it's not just technical skills and knowledge that matter for success. It's also the often-overlooked political skill that can play a significant role in navigating organizational landscapes, building influential relationships, and advancing one's career. This article delves into the importance of political skill at work, providing insights into navigating organizational politics effectively and discussing how to leverage it to grow your career.

Cindy has had many conversations with individual contributors and managers who say, "I don't want to engage in politics." That's just not possible in leadership. It is somewhat possible as an individual contributor, but to perform at your highest level, you still need to engage in politics. Let's look into why.

Understanding Political Skill

Political skill is the ability to read people at work and use that knowledge to get ahead, influence others, and achieve goals. It includes being socially aware, knowing how to persuade others, having a good network, and being genuine. It's not about being sneaky or untrustworthy but rather about being intuitive, resourceful, and authentic in your interactions.

The Four Dimensions of Political Skill

Yes, there are **four** official dimensions of political skill. Let's review them:

1. **Social Astuteness** - The ability to observe and interpret social situations accurately.
2. **Interpersonal Influence** - The capacity to persuade and influence others in a way that seems natural and genuine.
3. **Networking Ability** - The skill to develop and maintain a broad network of contacts.
4. **Apparent Sincerity** - Appearing honest, open, and genuine in all interactions.

Note that last one - apparent sincerity. This is one of the areas where political skill can go poorly. If you appear sincere but are not truly sincere, you risk significant harm to your reputation. When we hear negatives about organizational politics, it often comes from people who are not truly sincere in their interactions or use their political skill for personal gain. Use your skill for good and for the good of the organization, and you'll be just fine.

Why Political Skill is Important

Today's corporate and organizational work environments are pretty complicated. There are so many diverse interests, conflicts, and power structures that it can be tough to navigate. That's where political skill comes in. It's the ability to understand and address these complexities successfully that can make a significant difference in achieving your professional goals.

Building strong relationships is key to achieving this success. Political skill enables individuals to build trust-based relationships that can be maintained over time. It's about enhancing visibility and getting recognized for your contributions. Of course, being good at your job is necessary, but it's not enough. You need to have the political skill to increase your visibility and show others what you're capable of.

Additionally, conflict is inevitable in the workplace, but politically skilled individuals can navigate conflicts diplomatically, finding solutions that satisfy all parties involved. This ability alone, the ability to manage conflict in the workplace, can be an incredible value to both you and any organization you work for.

Finally, influencing decisions is vital to achieving success in organizations. Decisions aren't always made based solely on data or logic. They're often influenced by relationships and perceptions. Political skill allows individuals to influence these perceptions and decisions positively.

Navigating Organizational Politics Effectively

We shared that navigating the politics of an organization can be challenging, but it's a necessary skill for career success. Building relationships with key decision-makers and influencers can help you achieve your goals and make a positive impact in the workplace. Here are some tips to help you navigate organizational politics effectively and build strong relationships.

1. **Understand the Landscape -** Spend time understanding the formal and informal power structures within your organization. Identify key decision-makers, influencers, and the relationships between different groups and individuals.
2. **Build a Diverse Network -** Develop relationships across different levels and departments. A diverse network provides broader insights and more opportunities to influence.
3. **Listen and Learn -** Be an active listener. Understand others' perspectives, goals, and challenges. This understanding will enable you to interact more effectively and gain allies.
4. **Be Genuine -** While it's essential to be strategic, it's equally important to be sincere. Authenticity builds trust, and trust is crucial for effective political maneuvering. Remember, use this skill for good.
5. **Provide Value -** Be someone who others want in their network. Offer help, share knowledge, and be positively present in the workplace.
6. **Choose Your Battles -** Not all issues are worth addressing. Assess the importance of different issues and decide where your involvement will be most beneficial.

Using Political Skill for Career Growth

Now it's time to consider using political skill to help you in your career. This means using your abilities to advocate for your interests and goals without appearing arrogant. It also means aligning your objectives with those of your organization, finding mentors and sponsors to offer guidance and support, and managing your reputation effectively.

1. **Advocate for yourself -** Speak up for yourself and your goals. Demonstrate your capabilities through action and help.
2. **Align with Organizational Goals -** Ensure your personal goals and values align with your company's goals and values to be a valuable team member.
3. **Seek Mentors and Sponsors -** Use your connections to find mentors and sponsors who can guide you and help you when the time comes.
4. **Manage Your Reputation -** Your reputation in the workplace is a combination of your actions and others' perceptions. What people think of you matters, so make sure they think positively of you and your abilities.
5. **Adapt and Learn -** As you progress in your career, continue refining your political skills. Learn from your experiences and change your approach as needed.

> **Pro Tip: If your personal goals and don't align with your organization's, it might be time to plan an exit strategy. Especially as a leader, your role is to promote the organization's values and goals. If they conflict with your own, you are positioned to violate your own integrity. This is a sure sign that it's time to move on.*

Political skill is an important tool for any professional. It's not about manipulating or deceiving others but understanding how things work in the organization and using that knowledge to work more efficiently within the system. By developing political skill, you can navigate workplace dynamics much better, build great relationships, and enhance your career prospects. Don't try to become a political operator; instead, try to be politically savvy by using your insight, integrity, and influence to achieve success in your job and contribute to the organization's goals.

> "Hardships often prepare ordinary people for an extraordinary destiny."
> – C.S. Lewis

17

Navigating Challenges & Setbacks

You might have noticed that, throughout this book, we mention the importance of relationships. Having strong relationships, and not burning bridges, is the key to a successful career, particularly when you have to navigate a challenging situation or setback

Melissa was in a director-level role and was not looking for a new opportunity when one fell into her lap. A recruiter had reached out with a VP-level role at a small startup company.

Intrigued, she went on the interview and found that she clicked with the people, loved the brand's aesthetics and mission, and was intrigued by the opportunity to be more hands-on as part of a smaller team.

The title was a full two levels higher than her current role, with a salary increase to match. How Melissa handled this situation is important and would be hugely important later.

She spoke with her boss, explaining the situation and why she was having a hard time saying no to the opportunity. They had a sincere and open conversation, which resulted in her boss telling her that she would always wonder what would have happened if she had taken the role and that she should go for it.

Ironically, less than 18 months later, the startup was in Chapter Seven bankruptcy, as this was during the financial crisis of 2008.

Because she had left on good terms and had stayed in friendly contact with her former boss and colleagues, three months after the startup ceased operations, Melissa was offered a role back with her former boss.

It is important to never burn bridges and to nourish and maintain relationships with people who matter to you, personally and professionally.

The path to career success rarely follows a straight line. Challenges, setbacks, and unexpected detours are almost inevitable. However, how you respond to these obstacles can determine your ultimate trajectory. By adopting the right mindset and strategies, you can turn setbacks into opportunities for a more resilient and fulfilling career.

Let's look at some setbacks and challenges that are common.

Impostor Syndrome

Many leaders and high-performing professionals struggle with feeling like they aren't qualified or deserving of their status. The simple fact is that when you're growing, you're doing things you've never done before. You should frequently feel uncomfortable. You should feel like you're trying something new. But don't doubt that you've earned the right to be there.

First, recognize that impostor syndrome is a common experience, even among highly successful individuals. It's not a reflection of your actual competence but rather a psychological phenomenon. Then, challenge negative self-talk. Instead of focusing on perceived flaws or shortcomings, remind yourself of your accomplishments, skills, and experiences that have led you to your leadership position.

Surround yourself with trusted colleagues, mentors, or coaches who can offer encouragement, perspective, and constructive feedback. Share your feelings of self-doubt with them – you might be surprised to find they experience similar thoughts. View challenges and setbacks as opportunities for growth, rather than proof of your inadequacy. Embrace a continuous learning mindset and seek out new knowledge and skills. Speaking of continuous learning…

Embrace the Growth Mindset

One of the most powerful tools in navigating challenges is cultivating a growth mindset. This means viewing obstacles as opportunities for learning and development rather than as signs of failure. When faced with a setback, ask yourself:

- What can I learn from this experience?
- How can I use this to grow as a professional?
- What skills or knowledge can I gain to better prepare for the future?

Remember, everyone experiences setbacks. The difference lies in how you choose to perceive and respond to them.

Reframe Failure as Feedback

Instead of seeing failure as a definitive end, reframe it as valuable feedback. Analyze what went wrong, identify areas for improvement, and create a plan to address those areas. This process will not only help you overcome the current challenge but also equip you with the knowledge and skills to prevent similar setbacks in the future.

Build a Support Network

Surround yourself with people who believe in you and your potential. Connect with mentors, colleagues, friends, or family members who can offer guidance, encouragement, and a listening ear during difficult times. A strong support network can provide valuable insights, perspective, and motivation to keep moving forward.

Develop Resilience

Resilience is the ability to bounce back from adversity. It's a crucial trait for navigating career challenges. To cultivate resilience:

- **Practice self-care** - prioritize sleep, exercise, and healthy eating to maintain your physical and mental well-being.
- **Manage stress** - Find healthy ways to cope with stress, such as meditation, mindfulness, or spending time in nature.
- **Focus on your strengths** - Remind yourself of your past successes and the skills you possess that can help you overcome challenges.
- **Maintain a positive attitude** - Cultivate optimism and a belief in your ability to navigate through difficult situations.

Embrace Change and Adaptability

The business world is constantly evolving, and being adaptable is essential for long-term career success. Be open to new ideas, technologies, and ways of working. Embrace change as an opportunity for growth and innovation. By staying flexible and adaptable, you'll be better equipped to navigate unexpected turns in your career path.

Seek Out New Opportunities

Sometimes, a setback can be a sign that it's time for a change. Don't be afraid to explore new career paths, industries, or roles. Network with professionals in different fields, attend industry events, and continuously learn new skills to expand your horizons. By being proactive and open to new possibilities, you may discover unexpected opportunities that lead to even greater success.

> **Pro Tip: Remember, your career is a marathon, not a sprint. Find some silence and space to think about what you want and the moves you need to make to get it.*

There is no such thing as an overnight success, and anyone that you admire and hope to emulate has had their share of setbacks. Setbacks are not fatal; they are an opportunity to iterate and grow. Plan, adapt, grow, repeat.

"The secret of getting ahead is getting started."
– Mark Twain

18

Next Steps

Throughout this book, you've been on a journey of self-discovery, strategic planning, and skill development. You've dug into your unique values, crafted a compelling career vision, and armed yourself with the tools to tackle the complex world of leadership.

Setbacks and challenges are unavoidable, but they're not roadblocks; rather, they're stepping stones on your path to growth. By building up resilience, embracing a growth mindset, and cultivating a strong support network, you're all set to turn obstacles into opportunities.

Remember, your career is a dynamic journey, not a fixed destination. It's a canvas where you can paint your aspirations, skills, and experiences. It's a testament to your resilience, adaptability, and unwavering pursuit of fulfillment. As you move forward, keep refining your brand, expanding your skillset, and nurturing your network. Embrace challenges, knowing that they're springboards for growth.

Your Career Resilience Blueprint is more than just a guide; it's a testament to your potential. It's a reminder that you have the power to shape a future that aligns with your values, passions, and ambitions. With the insights and strategies outlined in this book, you're well-prepared to navigate change, overcome obstacles, and craft a career that's truly your own.

The road ahead may offer unexpected twists and turns, but armed with your resilience blueprint, you're ready to face them with confidence, grace, and unwavering determination.

So, what's holding you back? Take the first step today. Embrace the challenges, seize the opportunities, and design a future that's as unique and resilient as you are. We're rooting for you!

Are you ready to unlock your full potential? Start building your resilient career now!

References

[i] Ose Askvik, E., Van der Weel, F. R., & van der Meer, A. L. (2020). The importance of cursive handwriting over typewriting for learning in the classroom: A high-density EEG study of 12-year-old children and young adults. *Frontiers in Psychology, 11*, 550116.s.

[ii] (n.d.). *60+ career change statistics for 2024 [that you didn't know!]*. https://novoresume.com/career-blog/career-change-statistics

[iii] (n.d.). *Topic: Online and social media recruiting*. Statista. https://www.statista.com/topics/2727/online-recruiting

[iv] (n.d.-a). *25+ surprising networking statistics [relevant in 2024]*. https://novoresume.com/career-blog/networking-statistics

[v] *The strength of weak ties*. Stanford Report. (n.d.). https://news.stanford.edu/stories/2023/07/strength-weak-ties

[vi] (n.d.). *5 Personal Branding Tips for Your Job Search*. The Manifest. https://themanifest.com/digital-marketing/5-personal-branding-tips-job-search

[vii] 54 percent of employers have eliminated a candidate based on social media. time to clean up your feed (and tags) | inc.com. (2020, January 9). https://www.inc.com/melanie-curtin/54-percent-of-employers-have-eliminated-a-candidate-based-on-social-media-time-to-clean-up-your-feed-and-tags.html

www.ingramcontent.com/pod-product-compliance
Lightning Source LLC
Chambersburg PA
CBHW070544090426
42735CB00013B/3068